IT ALL BEGINS
WITH YOU

How to Rise Above the Odds, Overcome
Addiction and Live Your Dream Life

BEN LANG

Copyright © 2024 Ben Lang

ISBN 979-8-9893196-6-4 (paperback)

JM Publishing LLC

DEDICATION

I genuinely believe that life and events happen for a reason. There will never be a time when you are faced with what you are unprepared for (this goes for the special person in your life.) We only attract who we are, and if we are ever going to attract our soulmate, we have to become attractive to what we are looking for.

I'm not just talking about looks. Your soul, mind, heart, and energy must align to truly have all you ever desired in someone, and you must be willing to give first to receive. Throughout my trials, the good times and bad, I knew that once I was right within, I would finally find my soulmate—the person I can sum up in two words: my everything.

This book is dedicated to the person who saw greatness in me, believed in me, and took a chance despite my past. The one who gave her time, energy, space, and life to believe in my dreams. The one who trusted my vision so much that it aligned with her vision and walked away from what she knew and into the unknown. Today, I wouldn't be where I am if it wasn't for your sacrifices, your understanding, and, most importantly, your courage. My life has been complete since the day I met you, and my world has truly been a blessing.

This book is dedicated to my life partner, my soulmate, and my wife, Lisa Lang. It all begins with you.

Contents

For more information about Ben Lang scan here

INTRODUCTION

I f we look back to when we were younger, we were free, driven, loved, enjoyed life, and every day was an experience. Those days were defined by what we would be when we were older and all of life's possibilities (which seemed endless). Every one of us has a path we must walk on; it's our unique journey in life. Many call this destiny, or what we were placed here for (purpose).

Of course, for all of us, there are life's detours. While these detours are designed to get us to the promised land, often, we travel on those detours and never get back on track. Most of us have experienced uncomfortable moments in life to get to where we are today. As difficult as life was at the time or even now, what we go through is life's unique way of growing us into who we are called to be on this earth.

In fact, all those things are required if you will impact life as it was designed for you. An old saying goes, "When the student is ready, the teacher will appear."

Life is that teacher, and we are truly the students who must be ready for what life can teach us to reveal our greatness. This can begin the day we sit on the edge of the bed and genuinely ask, *"What is my purpose?" "Why is this happening to me?"* and *"Whose life will change if I overcome this moment?"*

Trust me, there's a world of people waiting for you to make it through your process to motivate them to get through theirs.

You are the catalyst to many dreams, goals, and life's accomplishments. But you first need to be that for yourself.

As someone who's fully recovered from drug and alcohol addiction, I can recall the last few years of my life——the pain, hurt, frustration, fear, worry, sadness, and guilt that comes with it; it all led me down a destructive path where I lost sight of who I was and how much meaning my life has. When we are at those low points in our lives, we can transform our minds the moment we begin to see how valuable we are. Sometimes, that comes in the form of the actual low point itself, support, friends, family, or simply the inner courage that drives you to greatness.

Yes, you have value. You are important, and you were born with a purpose unlike anyone else. While you may be going through something today that causes you to think otherwise, I'm telling you no matter where you've been, what you may have lost, or how low life can be at this point, you have the power to turn your life around, but it all begins with you.

CHAPTER 1

Finding Value in Adversity

"Each trial we overcome rewards us with a piece of life's ultimate puzzle: our purpose."
—Ben Lang

An African proverb says, "If there's no enemy within, the enemy without can do us no harm."

On this day, I stared at the ceiling, reminiscing about the last few years of my life, the great moments, the setbacks, comebacks, the losses, and wins that I had taken for granted. A sense of sorrow overtook me. Having lost it all again, this time in the worst way, the enemy on the inside was causing me tremendous harm.

Yes, I've had my share of ups and downs, a rollercoaster life since childhood that contributed to my lack of being grounded, strong, consistent, secure, and confident. Could I blame my parents and upbringing? Maybe. Could I blame the divorce that shattered my world? Possibly. Perhaps I could blame serving time in prison or the many other moments when I let myself down or failed.

Whatever the case, my life became a mirror of the inner battle I had going on then. When no battle raged, I won. Life was easy—cruise control. But I should have pushed harder in life during those times. I should have gotten ready.

Because once a battle did rage, I lost and lost big, buckling under every challenge that life threw my way. When I struggled, I struggled severely, not understanding how to cope with the pain or the pressures of life. This often resulted in what would become my addictions—drugs and alcohol.

Still, while pushing my addiction aside, I forged ahead numbly as if there were no problem. No problem that drugs and alcohol couldn't solve, anyway. I ignored the lessons that life was trying to teach me.

Life has a way of shielding our journey to greatness. It disguises itself in obstacles and circumstances designed for us to experience. Each trial we overcome rewards us with a piece of life's ultimate puzzle: our purpose.

We never know how and why things happen in life the way they do. Usually, when tragedy strikes, we are unaware of the years we've sown into it. Because life events don't just happen. Somewhere in our past, we were not disciplined, consistent, committed, strong, caring, loving, or forgiving.

Life usually does not make you pay a heavy penalty for the first offense. In fact, I don't think any initial violation does. Paying a hefty penalty is the compound effect of it and its weight due to years of neglect or continued putting off to the side. When you finally pay the penalty, it can be very heavy. However, if we are honest with ourselves, we can, at some point, trace it back to where it all began.

For me, just a few short years prior, I rose out of financial ruin, recovering from bankruptcy after losing my entire real estate portfolio and just about everything else I thought was valuable in life at the time. Now, driven by adversity, I was (by society's standards) "the comeback person," thriving, earning lots of money, and living "the dream."

I vehemently believe the hunger and drive for success are always present. What stops people most of the time is their "inner motor" (self-esteem, belief system). Something, some addiction, is always larger than their purpose, and it outweighs their self-esteem/belief system, which also causes them to lose hope in themselves. This ultimately becomes their demise. They can be addictions to anything, too—not just drugs. They can be to comfort, pain, suffering, excuses, the past, the future, success, women, men, etc. Whatever "it" is, it can become an addiction.

Once I understood the mechanics of addiction, I learned to shift my addictions, and when I did, whatever I set my mind on became a success. That, too, was an addiction. After bankruptcy, I worked hard, going after external things. I opened a real estate brokerage and a gym and honestly thought I was doing well.

> **There was this unwavering belief inside that once you are successful you will always be successful but for the majority of that high point I always seemed as though I was one step from falling off the edge.**

For most of that high point, I always seemed as though I was one step from falling off the edge. There was no real surety within myself. How many times can a person come back after a setback? How many times can a person get up after being knocked down? How many times can a person push forward when the weight of the world is on their shoulders and all seems lost?

Those were the questions I asked myself one day. This day was no ordinary day. I was all alone with my thoughts. No TV, phone, or laptop. Just four walls and a single mattress.

After realizing I was in rehab, the walls of life were rapidly closing in. The conversations with myself were pretty rough. In fact, looking back, I would *never* speak to anyone the way I was speaking to myself that night.

Was it justified? I would never know. In times of weakness and pain, we can become our worst critics, and grace is needed most during these times. Just like in prior years, I was only thinking about myself. Selfish. But I finally realized I needed help—someone to save me from spiraling out of control.

In life, you don't ask for help because you are weak. You ask for help because you want to be strong. Strong enough to overcome the challenges of life, strong enough to have the will to win.

Rehab

I vividly remember the drive to the rehab center. On the way there, no matter what my inner man said, it was hard to see that I was better than the position I was currently in. The appearance of life, grief, pain, and heartbreak all outweighed my drive. My addiction had finally gotten the best of me and taken over. There I was, defeated again.

Looking back, part of the process that sent me to rehab may have stemmed from losing my sister two years earlier when she was only twenty-nine years old. *As I said earlier "if we are really honest with ourselves we can at some point trace it back to where it all began."*

For me, I'm sure it began there. My sister represented love, and if you know what love is in human form, it's hard to figure out if you'll ever experience that again when it's gone. She was the most beautiful, loving individual I knew. I always looked up to the way she was able to make people feel important. It's what I strive to do every day going forward.

But she, like me, dealt with something that no one knew about. While she was loving toward just about anyone who crossed her path, she fought her own mental health challenges, one of which was self-love. The battle was so intense and powerful that she succumbed to her mental health issues.

When someone this close to you tragically ends their life, you start to question yourself: Could I have just moved my own nonsense out of the way and helped? What if I wasn't so stuck on what I was dealing with to see that she really needed my help? Why couldn't I have just been there that day? Surely, I would have been able to talk her out of it.

As difficult as this was, everyone has their time and purpose in life, but at that time, losing her was the beginning of my mass destruction.

Over the next few years, I pushed everyone and everything close to me away except drugs and alcohol. My love for drugs and alcohol became my escape from reality and grief. They made me feel better but worse at the same time. It took away the mental pain temporarily, but physically, I was falling apart. One thing is for certain,

> **If you don't ask life what your purpose is, it will teach you a lesson. If you ask life what your purpose is, it will teach you a lesson.**

As James Allen, British philosopher and pioneer of the self-help movement, once said, "Circumstance does not make the man; it reveals him to himself." So when they appear, they are not for us to quit, throw in the towel, or give up on ourselves. This is the time to realize that you have a destiny in life. As difficult as it may be, any adverse circumstances we experience during this time are simply trying to get our attention. It's life asking us to look for the cure within what we are going through.

If you want more and want to overcome, the only person who is coming to save you is you.

The difference between my sister and I was that she was bold enough to end it all when life became too much. Depending on how you look at it, perhaps her purpose here had been served, and there was nothing left for her to contribute to the universe. Whatever tortured her, she gave in to it.

But me, I just couldn't quit on life. Something deep down caused me to take the slower route. Maybe that delay was for me to find value within myself. To truly find purpose and impact. Although I was on my way to rehab, just maybe that was the reason.

CHAPTER 2

······································

The Call

*"At your lowest point in life, you must learn
how to ask for help. Not because you are weak
but because you want to remain strong."*
—Ben Lang

F or years, I (like most people) ran away from my true calling. People run away from a calling because they don't understand their impact on the world. They are afraid to stand up for it. They have yet to see the value of who they are and what they can do to empower something or someone—their purpose.

Looking back, I didn't know I had a purpose or that it existed. Usually, when we don't know that, we freely give up on life by discarding ourselves as though we are not worthy of life. I went through life thinking I had goals and things to accomplish, but they were very surface-level. My success with business hid the emptiness, pain, and fear. I had no solid foundation to stand on. The outward appearance fueled my drive, and because of that, I lived an unfulfilled life. Instead of finding what I wanted to accomplish, who I was, and what I truly desired to be, I had no actual goals or real-life purpose until I got the call.

I could only discover my purpose by going deep within, finding myself in a dark, empty place.

The call can be traced back to various life events that a person has never healed from or received help for. Much of it stems from our childhood, which we never discuss. Therefore, we are unable to fully grasp and understand trauma when it manifests.

But holding in our emotions about our past distresses does more damage than good. We carry these disturbing experiences into our adult years, where anxiety, depression, and fear serve as reactions to what we saw, how we felt, and what happened to us.

Tragic life events happen, such as losing a loved one, a job or business shutting down, a marriage falling apart, or the complete loss of your physical ability to do what you were accustomed to doing prior. Such traumatic occurrences can drive us further into darkness, which can lead to addiction *before* losing it all (as in my case), or you can fall into addiction afterward. If your addiction occurs "before" the chaos becomes unbearable, the dependency begins slowly; then, gradually, you need more of it. You deny you have a problem because you can't see the internal battle now showing outwardly. Little by little, you start to lose your hold on what's holding you.

Becoming addicted to something afterward means you are so ashamed of who you've become that you need an escape. You need something to depend on because you cannot rely on yourself. You have let yourself down so many times. Your heart has been broken into pieces, and you are far away from being the person you once dreamed you would become as a child.

Both require you to look in the mirror and understand that your only enemy is the one on the inside. When you can defeat the enemy on the inside, the one on the outside cannot do you any harm.

When we are going through a battle and life is rough, we never think for a moment that the battle is not necessarily about us.

The battle is not to break you so you can quit. *The battle is for you to overcome because of the lives we will*

change and impact due to the very thing someone is facing. This is purpose. Purpose is impact.

There are three types of people in life: One is getting ready to go through what you've overcome. The second is going through what you've overcome, and the third has been through what you've overcome but is wrestling with the trauma of what has transpired and can't seem to move forward. This is what I mean by purpose.

While it may seem as if some of our life experiences are tragic, when we can transfer those experiences into our "whys," life becomes much more meaningful for ourselves and others.

The Fork in the Road Question

By the time I made it to rehab, I had lost every possible thing I could imagine. I had no hope; I was at my wit's end. The walls at the rehab center were closing in as I lay alone, trying to figure out how my life turned out this way. Just yesterday, I was thriving with successful businesses, money, and the life most people wanted. Now, it was my darkest moment; failure was my only feeling.

But as bad as my current state seemed, something inside of me still wanted to try for better. As I found myself in my deepest despair, a small voice asked, "Did you truly ruin your life? Is this really over? Or could this be the biggest turnaround from the lowest of low points?"

There it was, the **Mind Battle**.

> **The Mind Battle is when you know you are better than what and where you are but you failed yourself and you know it.**

The *Mind Battle* occurs when you know you are better than what and where you are, but you've failed yourself. Life feels like more of a loss than a win. There's nowhere to turn, and every door is closed. You are all alone with your inner thoughts and self-talk; if you are not careful, your negative self-talk will win.

That day, whatever small flame I had left was enough for me not to admit defeat entirely.

This is the "aha moment." The moment when you must make a choice, the moment when you must decide, "What do I really want for my life?" And when you answer, dare to see yourself at the highest point mentally, although you are at your lowest point physically. This is where all the excuses for why you are not living your most extraordinary life have to be removed. There are no more excuses, no more detours, and no more doing it tomorrow.

You are staring at the only person who can help you.

YOU.

This is the moment of decision. Either you will step back into safety or step forward into greatness.

Stepping back into safety is succumbing to life, feeling hopeless and powerless. Believing that you are not valuable and don't have a purpose. Every successful and unsuccessful person has been here before.

On the contrary, stepping forward into greatness is creating the life of your dreams, telling yourself, "As tough as a road that this may be, I know what I desire. I know this will be difficult, but I am worth it. My family is worth it. My purpose is worth it." You are finally taking the risk and betting on yourself.

The successful person believed that if you look at life as it could be and all its possibilities, it will become as it should be. The unsuccessful person continued to look at life as it was, and it only worsened.

The Life-Altering Question

George Benard Shaw, the Irish playwright, was asked while he lay on his deathbed, "If you had your life to do over again, what would you do differently?" He responded, "I'd be the person I could have been but never was."

We often reflect on how we'd live our lives over if given a new beginning. What we don't remember is that we have a chance to make a new beginning every day, with new and better choices. We just have to remember to take charge.

Someone asked me a similar question on the first day of rehab:

Who would be at your funeral if you died today? Would they have any nice things to say about the life you lived? How many people would say you truly impacted them to be the greatest versions of themselves?

I wasn't on my deathbed, although it seemed as if life was pushing me pretty close to it, but this life-altering question became the turning point for me. I had to sit there and really think about my broken relationships, my failed businesses, my difficulty with having the right partner in my life, my lack of friendships, my sister's death, and how I really did not believe I could trust myself. Most importantly, my relationship with my daughter was destroyed.

As difficult as my life was, compounded with the amount of shame I carried, I knew the only person who could turn things around would be me, not anyone else. The pressure was enough to have another breakdown in rehab. The memories alone can cause anyone to suffer.

This is where self-talk becomes important, and if you have anything left to give, now is the time to pull yourself together. I had to stand, look in my mental mirror, and say, "You are the only one I can't fool anymore, and the fact that you still have life in your body means there's more life for you."

Whenever we have these breakdowns, the biggest challenge comes from not having enough positive emotions and self-talk saved to withdraw from our accounts. Our accounts are low and have negative balances. In these times, we must pull from the beliefs of others until our own beliefs kick in again and we have faith in ourselves.

The setback and adversity don't matter. All we need to know is that we can get through it.

The Mental Mirror

If you have ever been in a place where you felt defeated or as if life has taken its toll on you, it may be challenging to see yourself in a better position than where you are now. There is simply too much negativity and chaos obstructing your view. You can only see what's in front of you, not beyond.

The good news is what's in front of you is only as large as *you* are making it seem. To overcome it, you truly must take on one thing at a time. With every ounce of strength you have inside you, I want to challenge you to do one thing today—start! You don't have to be great to start, but you do have to start to be great.

So start envisioning a stronger, better, smarter you. A whole, healed, happy, positive you. Start to see that you can do or be whatever you desire. Of course, it will require that you do something you've never done before, especially to have what you've never had before. What you have currently is based on what you have been doing in the past.

To change your future requires you to change this moment.

Knowing my position was an uphill battle, I started with small steps. The most significant step to take is seeing yourself as the greatest version of yourself. Do that by defining who that person is, what that person has, and what that person does. Taking the limits off means there are no restrictions on the person you are building. Don't be afraid to write this person down as if it were impossible for them to fail at anything. Just like your favorite actor, entrepreneur, athlete, motivator, musician, influencer, or whomever you look up to—you too can be that.

Today, let's start with a simple exercise:

1. Write down three things you are grateful for.

2. Write down two important tasks you want to accomplish. This can be meditation, exercise, prayer, reading, or listening to something positive for yourself daily for 20 minutes.

3. Verbalize one affirmation per day. If you don't have an affirmation, you can start by saying, ***"Every day, in every way, I am getting better and better because I believe in myself."***

······· ·

CHAPTER 3

Although I've Been Knocked Down, I'm not Knocked Out

"Life is asking a series of questions that haven't been asked before. In the last few rounds of a fight you have to believe you can win, then come back and win it."
—Ben Lang

February 11, 1990, would be one of the biggest turns of events in sports history. The undisputed heavyweight champion of the world, Iron Mike Tyson, versus the heavily assumed underdog, James "Buster" Douglas. Many knew (based on Iron Mike's knockout history and the pace he was on as the heavyweight champion of the world by devouring opponents) that Douglas would be an easy win for him. He simply didn't stand a chance. So much so the odds were 42 to 1 in favor of Iron Mike.

At the time, James Buster Douglas wasn't even the number one contender; he was actually number seven, which made this fight even more of an easy show for one of the greatest boxers in the history of boxing. It would be a quick payday for not just Tyson but all the betters in this fight.

The two glared at each other. It was textbook Tyson to put fear in his opponents before the bell rang. Tyson took this fight as a joke; he took Buster Douglas as a joke.

In the first few rounds, Buster Douglas fought like he wanted to win. It was not going to be just another knockout. Tyson landed ferocious shot after ferocious shot, and the oohs and aahs of the crowd could be heard every time a punch landed.

But Douglas had a strategy. He knew he had a small window in which he could not fail. One wrong move, and it was over for him. Although he took brutal hits round after round, something inside him said, "I don't have anything to lose, and if I am going down, I'm not going down without giving you everything I have."

It wasn't just Tyson who believed this would be a quick fight. His cornermen were caught unprepared, too. They didn't bring the necessary equipment in case Tyson was injured, such as ice packs or the eye iron (in case the eye swells). Once Tyson's eye started swelling, they filled a rubber glove with ice between rounds.

Confusion and panic grew in his corner as the fight went on. Despite Tyson's inability to execute an effective fight plan, his corner continued to give him the same advice between rounds to move his head, jab his way inside, and deliver a right hand.

In the eighth round, Douglas dominated until the last few seconds. Within the last ten seconds of the eighth round, Tyson, who had been backed onto the ropes, landed a big, right uppercut that sent Douglas to the canvas.

The crowd stood to its feet. The referee, seemingly not getting to the knockdown count fast enough, was heard saying, "One, two," and then "Six, seven..."

As a shock to the crowd, Buster Douglas rose to his feet, more powerful than before. ***"Although I got knocked down, I'm not knocked out,"*** his persistence said.

The bell rang.

In the tenth round, Tyson pushed forward. However, he was still seriously hurting from the accumulation of punishment he had absorbed throughout the match and the lack of treatment from his corner. As Tyson advanced, Douglas measured him with a few jabs before landing an uppercut that snapped Tyson's head upward, stopping Tyson in his tracks. As Tyson reeled back, Douglas immediately followed with four punches to the head, knocking Tyson down for the first time in his career.

One of the greatest fighters of all time would go on to lose his title to one of the biggest underdogs in the most notorious upset in the history of sports. The fight would be talked about for decades after.

You Can Come Back from This

Life can be compared to the Mike Tyson versus Buster Douglas fight. Life is Big Bad "Iron" Mike Tyson. Ferocious, overpowering, and intimidating. We are coming in as the heavily favored underdogs. Adversity, trials, and setbacks hit us. While we were never given the road map to train for the life fight or the journey through it, we must realize (despite the odds being stacked against us) that no matter the rank in life, we are champions. Being a champion means believing in ourselves when all seems lost, e.g., being down to our last ounce of gas and getting ready to throw in the towel.

You get back up because life is worth fighting for. It means giving yourself that one last push, the push beyond quitting. Yes, people will give up on you, and doors will close to what we may have believed life should look like.

But this is life. Life is a game. It's a fight, and those who win strategize during adversity.

There will be moments that seem as though life has it out for us, and our only escape is to numb the pain. To fill the void with what may seem like a solution that only further damages us. In these moments, the voids become letdowns, which turn into even more unbearable circumstances. Then life continues to throw hit after hit, landing shot after shot.

Here is where we must trust in the belief that something larger than us exists. We must believe that we can overcome anything, no matter how many times we have been knocked down.

If we are not knocked out, we can get back up and win.

Buster Douglas knew he had nothing to lose. For myself, by the time I got to rehab, lost, broken, and afraid, feeling as though life got the best of me, I knew I had nothing to lose. You, too, may be at a place in your life today where you feel you're at the end of the rope and are a second or two away from the referee calling the fight. I encourage you: the fight is not over. You can come back from this. ***Your circumstances are not your conclusion.***

It's not final. No matter what has transpired in the rounds before. No matter what it looks like right now, every day (just like every round) at the lowest of lows, you must convince yourself that: "Although it seems as if I am an underdog in this life fight, I am bigger than what I am facing. I believe in myself more than I believe in adversity. There is *nothing* I can't come back from and win."

Turning the Fight in Your Favor

The law of cause-and-effect states that every effect has a specific and predictable cause. As we know it, every cause has an effect. Most people never live their purpose and achieve their dreams because they spend too much time fighting the circumstances. They find themselves fighting the appearances of life—what I refer to as "fighting effects with effects."

Our mistake is the amount of time spent fighting the effects instead of changing the cause of the effects—which is us. The most pivotal moment for me in rehab that I must share is this:

The secret to changing your life is to focus all your energy not on fighting the old you but building a new you.

The moment we look at life and our circumstances differently, life and our circumstances become different. The moment we change the cause (us), we change the effect.

Today, I want you to ask yourself these questions:

1. Who do I really want to be?
2. What do I truly want to have?
3. Where do I desire to go in life?
4. What do I want to accomplish?
5. Who will be proud of me for accomplishing it?
6. What legacy do I want to leave behind?
7. What will this world look like because I gave it the best version of me?
8. If I had the chance to live my life over, what would I do differently?

It's okay if you don't have the answers to those questions right now, but I encourage you to take some time and really think about them. The moment you answer them, get up at once and go after building a new you.

But remember to give yourself grace. Don't be so hard on you. No one is ever at their goal level when they first state what they want to accomplish, and some people are at the lowest point in their lives. However, they can see beyond what is apparent to the eyes.

This is why it's important not to blind yourself by who you are right now. If you do, you hold yourself hostage to what you could be.

I'm reminded of the baby elephant, who, as a baby, would be chained to a stake in the ground. The stake was attached to a chain that was only three feet long.

As the elephant grew older, it would continue to be tied to the same stake in the ground with only three feet of chain. The elephant is one of the most powerful creatures in the world. It can pull a train with people on it, but a small, flimsy chain trained his mind to think of himself as small, and because of it, the elephant remained a hostage. If it only knew how strong it was, how dominating it could be, and how it could break the chain with the swing of its leg, being bound would never be an issue.

The trouble lies in how long the elephant was conditioned to think of himself as less than, and that's the same trouble we face—being bound to the chains of life. If we knew how powerful we really are, nothing in this world would be able to stop us. All it takes is one moment for us to realize our power.

No matter where you are right now, find a mirror and look at yourself. Know that you are more than enough despite your reflection. You can have, be, and do all the things you can imagine, but you must imagine them without limits. Remember, no one in this world just got up and accomplished their goals the moment they said they would. It took time, dedication, commitment, passion, belief, and sheer determination to get there. It also took sheer willpower to know they wouldn't be held down by the chains of life.

Taking the first step to changing your life requires you to believe that it can be done. The next step is to take action. In order to stay committed and consistent, remember who you want to become and the life you want to live.

1. Like Mike Tyson, has there ever been a time in your life when you felt that continuing to show up unprepared is an automatic victory for you? If so, how long did that last, and what lesson did you learn?

2. When things are going well, do you:
   a) work harder
   b) slow down a bit
   c) stop showing up

3. Has there ever been a time when you were not prepared for the life knockout? This could be anything. What did you do to recover? If you didn't recover from it, how are you handling life now?

4. If you looked in the mirror today, knowing the real you, the one you can't hide from, what advice would you give yourself?

5. Have you ever given yourself grace? If not, today is the day to start.

CHAPTER 4

· ·

The Morning Routine

"To create the life of your dreams, you
must first decide and then take action. The
action becomes routine, the routine becomes
a habit, and the habit becomes your life."
—Ben Lang

There's a great book by William E. Bailey called *Rhythms of Life*. In it, he talks about a man who cried and pleaded with the universe for more time. He said, "Please, all I want is more time." The universe responded, "I can't give you more time; there is no more. Give me more of you."

We all have twenty-four hours in a day to create the life of our dreams, and that allotted time does not change. Here is what can change: YOU. We can't change past frustrations, events, or anything behind us, and the truth is that it doesn't matter what happened. What matters is what we do when we realize this is not how we want life to be.

The sum of our past is what and who we are today. However, this is not a bad thing. It's an experience we can use moving forward by giving more of ourselves in the same twenty-four hours.

To create the life of your dreams, you must first decide and then take action. The action becomes routine, the routine becomes a habit, and the habit becomes your life.

You may be thinking, *Well, you have no idea what I am facing. It's overwhelming, overpowering, and just too much to bear.* Life can very well feel like that. Especially when there is no image or picture of what you want it to feel like. This is why it's important to answer the questions in Chapter 3. They will help you create the image of who you want to be.

When most people are down and out, they have created a pattern for themselves. This pattern is formed out of their memory. It's based on their past experiences with moments of guilt, shame, frustration, and letdown. This pattern was created from a decision and then an action.

That action became a routine, and the routine became a habit. The habit became our life.

Anything that happens in life can be traced back to the choices that defined our habits, good or bad. Therefore, the only way to break the pattern is to decide what you want more: ***being down and out or up and winning***.

A lot of our hitting rock bottom stems from mismanagement. To excel to higher heights in life requires better time management. This is why Wiliam E. Bailey stresses the importance and power of time. If you mismanage your time, you can never get it back, but when managed properly, you can alter your life dramatically. That's all everyone ever really wants: the time to correct our errors and get it right.

Whenever we mismanage anything, we will lose it eventually. For instance, when we mismanage our health by not taking care of ourselves, we become sick and overweight. Mismanagement of our relationships causes painful breakups, and mismanagement of our money causes loss, poor credit, and other financial disasters. The mismanagement of our business or career results in failure and lost income.

In the same way, if we mismanage our belief in our abilities or how we see ourselves, we will hit rock bottom.

Therefore, the key to turning our life around is new management.

While in rehab, I began to change my life's perspective. I managed the questions I asked of myself. I managed how and what I felt about myself. But ultimately, I managed my emotions as well as what I believed in.

There were two questions I asked life:

1. Why do some people create the life of their dreams, finding happiness, love, and what they desire while making it look easy?
2. Why do other people never discover their purpose, do everything they desire, or live the life of their dreams?

Everyone has a choice about what to do with their time in life. What separates people is *knowing* what it is they should do. They do not have a goal or understand where they want to end up. Both people have the same twenty-four hours in a day, but one is pulled by purpose, and the other is pulled by reacting to what happens in life.

Then I asked myself, *How can I create the life of my dreams moving forward?*

I had to learn how to manage myself, becoming aware of who I am, what I desire in life, where I want to go, and what my goals are. It also meant understanding my mental, physical, emotional, and spiritual well-being. Much like a car, I had to recognize when I was running on empty and needed to be refueled instead of feeling sorry for myself and then further hurting myself by using drugs and alcohol to take away the guilt.

The truth is it's not easy to start making changes when you're accustomed to "living life." Living life on autopilot doesn't necessarily mean we check in with ourselves. Nor does it mean we know how to take care of our minds, souls, and bodies when we do run empty and break down at some point. Once we reach our breaking point, we must ask ourselves, "Why am I doing what I'm doing? What is the purpose of it? How does this contribute to my well-being?

Thinking Correctly about Ourselves

Take a moment to review your answers in Chapter 3. This time, rethink the questions with the mindset that you can't fail. ***It's having the I can mindset not the I can't mindset.***

Do not worry about what other people may think. What's more important is what you think. Worrying what others may think is one of the main reasons we don't live a life of fulfillment. We are always looking to ensure everyone else is okay with what we think and do, which is why many people don't accomplish their dreams freely. Either we feel as though we don't quite measure up to the standards of others, or we're overly concerned about their opinion of our decision to fulfill our purpose.

> **Quit spending time thinking about why you can't control. The reasons may be valid, but throw them all away. They are not doing you any good.**

Yes, the odds may be stacked against you, making it seem like winning is not an option right now. Nevertheless, today, I want you to quit spending time thinking about why you can't live the life of your dreams. It's pointless. Instead, think as if you could have everything you desire, become who you want to be, and do anything in life.

Think with the perspective of not caring what anyone else has to say.

Most of the time, when we answer questions about who we are, what we want to be, do, and have, we answer them from a limited thought process. Our answers reflect how we feel about life at that precise moment. But how would we feel if we didn't have to deal with what's in front of us first? Or hear critiques from people when we choose to break free?

> **We experience life according to what we believe about ourselves.**

We will not rise to higher heights until we begin to think correctly and clearly.

The Greatest Investment

Warren Buffet, one of the wealthiest men in America, was asked, "What is the greatest investment you could ever make?" He answered, "The greatest investment we could make is the one we make in ourselves."

He meant that investing in ourselves is not about money only but what we invest in terms of time, energy, spirit, physical, and mental health. One of the most important things successful people do is surround themselves with everything they need to operate at a high level of success. This is how you invest in yourself.

Investing in ourselves means everything could be lost, but that would never concern us as we have the tools and principles to make a comeback. This way of thinking is very different from the person who believes that once they are down, they are down for good.

Think of it this way—anything you invest in will (to some degree) produce a return. When you spend time, energy, or money, your mindset is a return on your investment. We must live and create our lives as if they are investments.

> **Successful people realize they are either creating a life by design or living a life of guilt.**

Creating a life by design means you are living on your terms. You know what outcome you want for yourself; you are the architect of your life. While every day has its challenges, ups and downs, you remain constant because you are painting the beautiful picture of the life you want. You realize that when you change, everything changes for you. You are proactive, not reactionary.

One of the things I started while in rehab (which I still do to this day) was my daily morning routine. It has been the reason my life has changed dramatically. I consistently read, listen to motivational messages, use positive affirmations, meditate, review my goals, and work out. This is one of the most essential yet overlooked strategies because it requires you to focus on yourself first. Carving out time every day before your day starts is a non-negotiable when investing in yourself.

Understanding the importance of setting aside blocked-out time in the morning to supercharge before taking on the world is vital, or else you will allow the world to take on you.

The truth of the matter is everyone has unplanned circumstances and adversity. No one is exempt from them; that's a given. However, what separates successful people from those who are not is they are fully equipped to overcome challenges because they have a proven system to take care of themselves first. They will perform well and meet their goals with a morning routine to start their day. That's the power of being prepared.

Not being our best means being unable to pour from a full cup, and years of this leads to a life of guilt. When we live life with guilt, it's because we regret not doing what we know we should. This puts us in a position to beat ourselves up for not living on our terms. Instead of returning to school or starting a business, we didn't give ourselves a chance. We remained in comfortable chaos because we didn't think we could.

That's guilt. It's your reaction to what happens after you've experienced upsets, and now you constantly allow circumstances to move you instead of moving the circumstance. Each day, you are being pulled in every direction except the one you truly want.

I encourage you to evaluate your morning. How do you start your day? If you don't have a morning routine and want to change your world, look no further. Here is where you must start. This is the most critical step.

If you don't have enough time in the day, get up earlier. For example, get up at 5:00 a.m. instead of 7:00 a.m. It will give you two extra hours a day, 35 hours a week, and 1,680 hours a year. You are important, and the time you commit to yourself is much more valuable than the time you devote to anything or anyone else. While those two extra hours may not seem dramatic from the onset, try it for one year to see where you are with your dreams, goals, and new life. You deserve to give yourself this.

If you don't have a morning routine, ***try this with me for the next 30 days:***

1. Set a goal—something that you have always wanted to achieve that you quit on, never did, or it was just a wish because you felt it was too hard to accomplish.

2. Refrain from speaking negatively of yourself in any way. Instead, say positive affirmations.

3. Stop thinking about all the reasons you can't accomplish this goal and instead focus on all the reasons you can.

4. Trace your attitude about accomplishing goals back to your childhood, and think about when you stopped believing you could accomplish goals.

5. Change the image you have of yourself by writing out a description.

6. Every day, act like the person who accomplishes the goal you created for yourself.

CHAPTER 5

· ·

You Are Not the Problem

"Life doesn't make problem people;
It makes people capable of handling problems."
—Ben Lang

Have you ever thought, *I just can't help being who I am?* Maybe you even believe the choices you make are who you are. The fact is, you can help being who you are—and become who you want to be.

The moment you begin to recognize that you and you alone are responsible for your life, you have the power to chart your own path. You have the power to make your own choices about your life and all that you desire.

Before you can move forward and begin building the life of your dreams, I want you to separate yourself from your past wrong conclusions. Those things are no longer what or who you are. Instead, believe that you can and will make the right decisions from this day forth.

Right decisions come from right ideas. Remember the life you want to live? The person you want to be? The legacy you want to leave behind? Those are the right ideas about you and your future. Your past ideas about life and yourself have brought you to this point. Now that you have changed that way of thinking, your new ideas about yourself and life will take you to the new heights you dream of.

As quoted in the beginning of this chapter, *"Life doesn't make problem people; it makes people capable of handling problems."* This means you have the power and ability to overcome any problem you may face. Yes, problems may seem difficult. However, they are only difficult because you don't realize you can solve them. You may have given up at the first sign of a setback or adversity because that's where your mindset is. You were probably thinking, *I'm defeated*, but that's not the truth.

There's no dead end to a problem, just a dead end in the way We are thinking about them.

When you know the truth, it sets you free. Free from the lie that you are hopeless, lost, and can't recover from the circumstances you are facing. What is that truth? That you can have, be, and do all that you ever dreamed of. You can overcome all things. Sure, life has taken its toll on you. It has for many of us, but you now have the experience to pay that toll, cross the bridge, and dream on.

The key words are "dream on." Most people hold on to their issues; they keep their problems glued to their brains. They can't wait to talk about them to whoever will listen, and when they don't have anyone to vent to, they talk about it to themselves. But nothing negative will go away if we always give it our full attention. We think about it, feel it, and then think about it more—then feel it even more. Anything we focus on stays in our conscious mind.

On the other hand, what we no longer give attention to, leaves. However, more attention must be directed toward something greater than our problems—progress.

Unfinished Business

Recently, I found myself intrigued, watching a story about a hippo being attacked by a crocodile. The attack was subtle. The hippo was just enjoying the day and submerged himself in the water. Most times, crocodiles go weeks and sometimes months without food. By attacking this great, big hippo, the crocodile was brave or desperately needed to eat. Crocodiles know they aren't much of a match for a hippo, especially a full-grown one, and they tend to go in another direction if they see them.

From the onset of the attack, it looked as though the crocodile would take down the hippo, but he could not do the death roll that takes most prey out. A crocodile's death roll involves biting, locking into their prey, and spinning them around. But this big hippo decided to fight back; it knew its life would not be over, and definitely not to some crocodile. In many other predator-prey cases, the hunted can only fight back for so long, but usually, it's not a good ending for them.

However, within a few seconds, life would change for the struggling hippo and the crocodile. Another hippo saw the tussle and immediately rushed in to save the hippo, then another one, then another one, and then another one. Out of nowhere, a gang of hippos came in to save their family member, tossing the crocodile like a beach ball.

Just like that, the circumstances changed. What was once an almost tragic moment for the hippo became a life lesson. The original hippo, who was initially being taken down, was now an active participant in the tossing of the crocodile as well.

**You are no observer of your life. You are
an active participant.**

A turn of life event can happen swiftly and in any
direction. The crocodile, once the aggressor, now finds
himself in big trouble, and from the looks of it, a big lesson
was learned that day: **Don't mess with the big bad hippo.**

At that point, I realized this is what believing in
ourselves means. Life can attack at any moment. Usually, it
attacks when we least expect it—when everything is calm,
some of it from way out of left field. But just because life
looks a certain way and can seem like it's getting the best of
us, ready to take us over, it doesn't mean life is over.

The difference between the people who win and those
who don't is that the winners ***know that no matter their
negative circumstances, there is a protector.*** They have a
support system that will save them if they believe in it and
become an active participant in the journey. This translates
into "Ask for help." We can't do everything by ourselves.
Active participants don't just *believe* it's going to happen, get
better, or turn around. They work like it's going to happen,
get better, and turn around. And ultimately, it will.

You decide your outcome by what you believe.

**Life can be against you if you look at it
that way or it can be for you. You decide
by what you believe.**

In this case, all of our mind, spirit, and physical help kicks in. Creating positive results in your mind first highlights the importance of daily meditation, working out, praying, and focusing on your dreams and goals. You must believe that when life looks like it's overtaking you, you can fight back and overcome it.

Like the crocodile and hippo, life takes you off course when you least expect it. Our faith lets us know our power and purpose; the odds against you won't matter. In our most challenging moments, life's reinforcements will come in at the last second, and as long as you know there is unfinished business, you will win.

The Decision is on You

Today is the day to make a decision. To decide is one of the biggest challenges most people face. However, choosing to be happy, loving, move on, and forgive the past, ourselves, or even perhaps how life looks at the moment is essential.

The opposite of decision is indecision. Indecision keeps people on the sidelines; it causes procrastination and prevents people from taking ownership of life. Indecision allows circumstances to grow gradually until they become difficult to work through. If you trace your steps back to the starting point of how you got to where you are right now, I can assure you it was because of indecision.

Indecision is a decision; it's just a decision to fail.

When a farmer plants his seeds in the ground, he knows what he planted, so he knows what he will manifest. He waters the ground and keeps the birds and pests away. He does this without seeing any results initially because he believes that if he does the daily activities religiously, he will eventually see what he planted.

It's a long journey. However, he knows he must wait and faithfully tend to the garden. If he gets in a hurry and digs up his garden to check the seeds' progress, he kills them due to impatience. He not only has to have faith, but he must be patient and believe in the process until the harvest appears.

He also has to make the decision to trust what he plants. As long as he does the work, he will reap. It may be an uncomfortable time, but it's worth the wait, and the farmer has trained himself.

This is where the critical role of decision-making comes in, along with deciding to be patient during the process. As I previously stated, you can decide to stay as you are, or you can decide to be uncomfortable for a while and push forward into the life of your dreams. But you must form a vision of what you want and make the decision to act upon it.

Most people prefer comfort, ease, conflict, and troubles that magically disappear. So, while a new life sounds good to them, they fail to decide to go for it. Every person living the life of their dreams right now decided to adjust and maneuver around the discomfort. They decided to turn on the switch and become the person they once dreamed of then but are living now. Every successful and motivated mind began with the decision to become victorious. Just as every failed, unmotivated mind remains indecisive.

You have the power to determine your own experience by making the right decision. Just remember, indecision is a decision; it's just not the right one. When you realize the totality of possibility is within your grasp, you can envision what you want to be and have whatever you desire—as long as you believe it is possible. Successful people are no different than you, except they knew what they wanted and assumed they could do it. That assumption became the decision in which they put forth the effort to achieve their desired result.

You were not born to be an observer. You are an active participant in the universe. Don't ever let anyone (even yourself) make you believe that you are unimportant. God did not make a mistake when you were born. You were created to live in these times because you were equipped to meet the challenges that you are facing. You are the right person, in the right place, to create the right world for yourself. Even though it may not look possible, you are already equipped with everything you need to make the impossible possible, including the decision to do it.

We know now that life doesn't make problem people; it makes people capable of handling problems. So, let's revisit some areas in life that you may have thought were too much of a problem in the past.

1. Have you ever felt as if you were always the cause of something bad happening in life? If so, list the reasons you felt that way. Did you make any new discoveries about yourself after listing those reasons?

2. In the past, when you faced a problem, can you confidently say you've exhausted all your problem-solving abilities before you gave up, assumed it would just go away, or attempted to cope with the problem by becoming addicted to something? Please explain.

3. When life has an unexpected turn of events, do you allow life to take you down emotionally, physically, and spiritually? Or do you become an active participant in problem-solving?

4. How often have you been faced with a decision and chosen not to decide? What was the outcome of indecision?

5. Do you believe that you decide the outcome of your life based on your beliefs? Please explain your answer.

CHAPTER 6

You Can Be Happy if You Decide to Be

"We all should get to a point where happiness is a choice we make every day. It should not be an option based on happenings."
—Ben Lang

One day, I watched a goldfish swim around in a tank. Goldfish, in my opinion, are one of the most intelligent fish. They have exceptional memory and cognitive abilities. If you put them in a stimulating environment, it contributes to their overall well-being and mental stimulation. Consistent training, repetition of learned tasks, and reinforcement through positive rewards invigorate the goldfish's ability to remember and retain.

I thought, *There's no way God created this goldfish to be bored and unhappy. He knows he's a goldfish, doesn't complain about it, doesn't try to fit in, nor is he worried about his tiny tank. The goldfish does not worry about anything outside the tank; it's just him and his world. He enjoys life by keeping himself active. No pressure.*

The number of people today who are unhappy with life is shocking. Part of it stems from their false idea about what they should be doing and where they could be in life. Attempting to measure up to someone else is another reason for their discontent. When most people don't measure up or feel inferior, they do things to fill the void.

But the problem is, they have created a person they "think" they should be based on someone else's talents and abilities. Due to the enormous pressure of this false image and the fact that they don't measure up, they are victims of the "we are our own worst critic" scenario.

However, failure is not a person, nor should anyone consider themselves one. Failure is an event in our lives in which we don't make the right decision. So, if we want to change our failures, we must remove all harsh judgments from our mindset and work to correct the actions that produced the wrong results.

Like myself, whenever I faced down moments or didn't feel as if I measured up, drugs and alcohol became my companions. It was my failure. I began to spiral. The substances became my escape, my go-to. I didn't know I was suffering in silence, and my ego was too large to ask for help.

I did not know how deeply I was failing. If you asked me then why I resorted to drugs and alcohol, my response would have been, "It helps take away the pain." I didn't see myself correctly, and I didn't place value on my life. I just didn't know who I was. Instead, I focused my attention on how to change events, situations, and conditions. I didn't think about myself.

Why? For years I carried a label about myself. As a child, I heard and saw some things from my parents and others. Growing up, I took that with me until I was an adult. I had no choice but to be that label, not realizing I was battling someone I was not until my rehabilitation.

As adults, when our worlds become a mess, we label it, and that's the standard we live up to. A label. "This is just who I am," we say and believe. Some of us have been labeled all kinds of things since we were children, and we carried those labels into our adult years. It never dawns on us that before anything in our life changes, we need to change our opinion of ourselves. No one else matters.

**Through my addiction, I carried a label
with me for quite some time. It's taken
me years of hard work and consistency
to get this label off my back.**

The label I carried with me was: although I looked good on the outside, things were not good on the inside. I was not happy.

Happiness Starts on the Inside First

What does happiness mean to you? Lots of money, being healthy, loving family and friends, finding someone special, traveling the world, buying a home for your children, returning to school, or supporting a charity or organization?

Forgiving someone?

Moving on from the past, letting go of fear?

It's important to understand that if we want to change our world, we must first exercise our faith by persistently bringing forth that change. We must learn to be happy with what we are working on until we get there. We do that by structuring and organizing what's around us—being intentional and persistent.

Persistence is another word for faith; if there is no faith, there is no persistence. This means believing in something so much that the action follows until we are the change we wish to see.

A changed experience can only happen to a changed individual.

Many times, people find themselves navigating through life as someone other than who they truly are. What's going on inside is being hidden by the outside until it all comes crashing down. These people live in the world as chameleons. They laugh at what others laugh at, eat, shop, watch, and listen to what they are told, and do everything other people do instead of what they truly desire. This is unhappiness personified, and they often don't realize this is not what they want to do or want to be until they hit a wall.

A changed experience can only happen to a changed individual. Know this: whatever you need to make you happy is at hand. Your perspective just needs to change. No longer can anyone say they are isolated or feel alone.

Take a look in the mirror and start there. You are God's perfect work. God's work in you has already made you wholly accomplished—it just needs your recognition and your belief. You are one of one, and make no mistake about it. Even if you are at what you perceive as your "rock bottom," you can still be happy; you can only go lower if you tell yourself you can.

We are so busy doing and worrying about so many things that we fail to nurture our minds with the right perspective and become unhappy with our circumstances. When we say we are unhappy, we give freedom for all the reasons for us being unhappy to come into existence.

Remember, no one can keep us from being happy but us.

Are You Bored?

One common factor that causes our unhappiness in life is boredom. Many people suffer from boredom and don't even realize it. Years ago, my life had become the same rat race day in and day out, and there seemed to be no escape. Work, home, bills, plus responsibility equaled the same routine.

It was not until I started a self-check or a weekly evaluation that I determined I was simply bored and stuck with my life. Just as jobs give evaluations for promotions or raises, we should evaluate where we are in life. Too many of us don't check in on us.

Check in with yourself today and see if you are bored with your life. Ask yourself: "Do I like what's going on right now?"

This is not a reason to go out and do something extreme as a means of escape. However, if you discover you are bored, that can be part of your negative mental and emotional state. If you find yourself bored too often, you will indulge in it, leading to a destructive mindset called "lazy thinking."

This is why it's essential to know that happiness is an inside job. With everything we have available in the world today, being bored makes absolutely no sense. There are interesting ideas, people, and events happening all around us daily.

Opportunities to create the life of our dreams are much easier to obtain today than they were years ago. The trouble with many people is their two perceptions.

One, their minds are like old-school record players. They play the same old way of thinking over and over. In their minds, the only good times in life were years ago. They review the past too often, thinking about the "good old times" and what they could or should have done. They prefer to rethink the past rather than to think about the present. They are bored. They complain but make no effort to rectify their situation.

The second perception is carrying unforgiveness for people, life, events, mistakes, and, most importantly, themselves.

We stand between the old familiar ways and the new and unfamiliar ways. And unfortunately, many would rather stay in a known hell than venture out into a strange heaven.

Check your thoughts over the last few days; this will show you where you stand in your mind. Be honest with yourself, whether it depresses you or makes you happy. We all must strive to get to the point where happiness is a choice we make every day. It should not be an option based on happenings.

The fact that you woke up today and are here is more than enough reason for you to be happy.

Life has its ups and downs. That's a given. While we may take for granted our time here on earth and our ability to wake up every day, today, going forward, instead of talking about everything or anything negative or going wrong, let's begin the process of gratitude and what's going well. This small change will dramatically transform our lives.

Thoughts on gratitude

1. Define gratitude and what it means to you.

2. What five things are you grateful for?

3. In thinking about what you are grateful for, list three reasons why you are grateful for them?

4. Is it possible to be grateful and happy at the same time as being negative and upset? Please explain.

5. Do you need something on the outside to make you happy, or does happiness start within? Please explain your answer.

6. If we want to create a changed experience in our lives, what must happen first?

CHAPTER 7

You Owe it to Yourself

*"You owe it to yourself to live
the life of your dreams."*
—Ben Lang

T he Children of Israel wandered through the wilderness for forty years before entering the promised land. During those forty years, the disbelievers and doubters died. They did not believe they could succeed in the promised land, so their mindset was: "Let's just return to what we know, even if it means being in bondage."

It was not until all the doubters were gone that the new generation was able to move forward in the promised land. ***Their decision produced their demonstration.***

"A Double-Minded Man is Unstable in All His Ways."
- James 1:8

The indecisive, hesitant, and fearful mind has made no impact in the world. Many live life constantly second-guessing themselves, doubting, feeling powerless, sorry, hopeless, as though they have no real value. This has caused them to exist but not fully live.

The biggest challenge that holds people back from their new life is giving too much time and attention to what they don't want. This focus keeps them from moving on. This is because giving attention to what you don't want keeps what you don't want around. No one wants to feel bad all day, drowning in sorrow, pity, worry, or fear. Not believing that they, too, have a promised land is what keeps them there.

We know we don't want to be where we are, but our mindset and environment have us trapped in a "This is all I know and what life has given me" attitude. We have all been down before, and focusing on our promised land can take a lot of mental work.

If your world represents letdowns, adversity, or situations where you feel you need to numb the pain, I encourage you to ask yourself: "What would happen if I use this moment to become the greatest person I could be? What would happen if I turned my life around and became a person of impact, a person of value, a person who could empower the same people dealing with the same challenges I'm faced with today?"

Self-Blame vs. Self-Understanding

Self-blame is much different than self-understanding. Self-blame causes destructive patterns. You are your own worst critic, constantly beating yourself up every time you look in the mirror, and you never can seem to get anything right.

The truth is, if we continue to search for all our many faults, we will continue to find them. We will never get it entirely right. No one is without fault, and once we understand that, we can take the pressure off ourselves and live a free life.

Self-blame is an unhealthy pattern that strips us away from our true potential and purpose. This causes us to walk around in guilt, which lessens our ability to be who we truly are.

Our guilt loads need to be lessened, not expanded.

73

We often create negative patterns throughout our lives that form a sort of conspiracy against us. Everything seems to be out to get you, and if you take a closer look at life, it seems just that way:

- I'm not happy.
- I'm not loved.
- No one cares.
- I'm sick.
- I'm broke.
- Business is slow.
- I'm overweight.
- My relationship is horrible.

The list goes on and on. Realizing that self-blame obstructs our creative process and removes us from seeing ourselves as God made us, which is in His perfect image. This is the first step toward learning that no matter where you are at this moment, you owe it to yourself to live the life of your dreams.

Self-understanding, on the other hand, is constructive. It's believing in the possibilities and moving onward and upward at all costs. It's knowing that, as Shakespeare once said, "There's nothing either good or bad, but thinking makes it so."

Self-understanding is a sign of healthy thinking. You realize you are the sum of your patterns, beliefs, and causes. And if things are not going right in our lives, we start with ourselves. The bulk of what we may be dealing with now should not be burdened with past mistakes or falsely perceived failures. They are of the here and the now, supported by the creativity of the past. This means that they are today's patterns, beliefs, and causes. You are at peace with them. They inspire, not conspire. You should feel as if you are a harmonious whole.

The challenge of life is to make the best use of what you have within you. That's the true definition of self-understanding.

You Owe It to You

American radio speaker and author Earl Nightingale once said, "Everyone is self-made, but only the successful person will admit it."

No one walks around saying they are a self-made failure or self-made quitter. They surely don't say, "I'm a self-made loser." Why? Because they don't believe that those effects are self-made. So, instead of self-understanding their actions and reactions, they blame the circumstances.

Blaming your circumstances and looking for sympathy can even make them worse. No one wants to hear someone complaining about their issues and problems and offer sympathy all day. Sure, things happen in life, and you have support, but constantly existing in a down-and-out position while complaining about it is a fast way to find yourself alone. In fact, the people who sympathize daily are also dealing with self-esteem issues that are possibly worse than yours. So, instead of motivating you, they'd rather hear your issues—not help. You do not sympathize with a successful person; you praise them.

There is nothing in a successful person's mental makeup to warrant sympathy.

You owe it to you today to decide to live the life of your dreams. Create new opportunities for yourself. Be the healthiest, happiest, loving, and most positive person you know. The decision to do this will pay off in rich dividends.

Believe it is possible to

- turn life around
- recover from any down-and-out circumstance
- triumph over constant fear

- replace worrying about your future with self-confidence in your future
- deal with sickness with faith and a proactive approach

Now, you are ready for that which is yet to be known. All your dreams, goals, and ideas are already in your mind and will appear on time and in order. From this day forward, you expect the unexpected in a positive way instead of with a negative outlook. You welcome it as each sign of your new life begins to appear. You expect health because you have no fear of illness.

All mental and emotional conflicts about who and what you are are gone.

The moment we plant the seed is not the moment we reap the harvest.

It may have taken you some time to find yourself where you are today. Perhaps years. That's okay. Today is a new day, and you owe it to yourself to plant new seeds.

I remember how they gave out packs of flower seeds in elementary school. Our job was to go home, get some dirt, and put the seeds in there. We knew what kind of plants they would be because they were on the package. All we needed to do to see them grow was do the work requested. Then, one day, the plant started to sprout.

You have the same power now as you did then. The difference is that you decide what you want your world to look like today. Write it, frame it, look at it daily, and work as hard as possible to materialize it. Most importantly, believe that you owe it to yourself to do the work so you will one day be truly self-made.

You owe it to yourself to live a life free of indecisiveness, hesitancy, and a fearful mind. None of these have any impact on the world. Now is the time to release yourself.

1. Write down three things you have been indecisive, hesitant, and afraid of. Be very honest with yourself.

2. With your response, why do you think you have been indecisive, hesitant, and afraid to do what you wrote down?

3. Do you believe that YOU have been holding you back or being indecisive, hesitant, and afraid? Please explain your answer.

4. If you were able to accomplish what you wanted without what you deem has been holding you back, how soon would you accomplish it? Explain.

CHAPTER 8

· ·

Decide Today

"Whoever you decide to be, make
sure YOU decide to be!"
—Ben Lang

What's the worst possible outcome of you changing your life right now?

I want you to consider this, because your outcome does not determine your worth. Neither does what your life looks like at the moment. It's what you do with the outcome that defines who you are.

Sure, you've had adversity, suffered heartbreak and drama, and felt you couldn't make it. We have all been there before to some degree. But you must understand that your hardships were not sent to destroy you. They were not meant to be ongoing battles to which you continue giving all your power and energy daily. That is not your label.

Instead, your hardships were for you to see that, as uncomfortable as it is, you must act as a new person to move beyond the moment. This new person thinks positively about themselves, life, and all its infinite possibilities. You must decide between being comfortable and down or temporarily uncomfortable on the way to the promised land.

Tests will arise; that's a part of the process. What we must realize is the test is for you to pass. Tests are not designed to break you. They are designed to measure you and determine whether you are ready for the next level. If we are not ready yet, the tests act as lessons for us to know what we need to work on.

The Next Level

One truth I have learned is we can't take possession of what we desire at our current level. If we could, we wouldn't desire it—we would have it.

Being down, depressed, broken, lost, bitter, and negative only attracts the same. No matter how difficult life gets, always see the circumstances you face as something you can overcome rather than something holding you back. Viewing life this way is your buoy through those hard times.

On the day I started writing down what I wanted to do with my life, I knew I couldn't reach my goals while at my lowest point. I also knew I couldn't continue feeling sorry for myself. Nothing I truly desired could possibly be attracted to me there. The only thing that would find me appealing was more of the same.

This is how the phrase "Every time I turn around, something is going on" came about.

Think about it this way: if like attracts like, how can you attract the good you desire while operating the same way you've been for years? You can't, and that's why you will continue to get what you've always gotten.

You must become the person that the life you desire becomes attracted to you.

This is the most challenging concept to grasp, especially when people feel as if life is after them, breathing them up and leaving them to declare, "If it's not one thing, it's another," and the list goes on.

The truth is, life's not out to get you. We live in a time when we can turn our lives around any time we choose. Our desire to begin on the path to our dreams will be set in motion the moment we declare the following:

1. "Enough is enough, I want to live."
2. "To live, I first have to give."
3. "Give more of myself to myself."
4. "Believe more in myself."
5. "Know that I can, and simply because I can, I will."

That small shift in our minds can radically change our lives almost overnight. It can be hard to think that way, but trust in your ability to choose.

> **While the results in life may be facts, the facts do not determine our lives— only we do.**

Make Sure You Decide to Be

As weak as I was walking into rehab years ago, I knew I had a purpose in life. I knew my mission was more important than the mess I was in.

When our lives look unfavorable, we can't walk around feeling sorry. Instead, we have to assess the damages. We assess the damage by seeing where life is at the moment and what can be salvaged or rebuilt. Some things need to be torn down completely. I needed help to end my self-pitying.

I thought about my sister's positive words to me and how much I'd miss her and my family. Then I thought about the lives I messed up because I wasn't operating at my full potential. Could I blame my mother and father? Could I blame the drugs and alcohol? Could I blame myself for being a failure by not being the best father to my daughter? Could I blame the divorce?

Sure, I could. That was partly why I was in rehab. I blamed everyone else and gave myself a pass for the life I was not living.

The facts were, yes, my life was a disaster. There was no disputing that. Here is what I decided to dispute: it no longer had to be that way.

Here's what I can dispute for you: your life can be greater than what it is now, even if you can't see it. All you need in life is to operate on someone else's belief until your belief kicks in. That's what rehab did for me, and this is what I am doing for you.

One morning, I woke up and did not feel like my usual self. I decided I didn't want to feel depressed, rejected, and like a failure anymore. I stopped focusing on those emotions and started focusing on what I wanted life to be. I turned my attention away from feeling down and out, and just like that, the feeling left. ***I decided to be.***

Whoever you decide to be, make sure YOU decide to be!

Whoever you decide to be, make sure YOU decide to be. This means to live life to the fullest and on your terms. Make sure you contribute to life by living in a way that will leave a lasting impact. Make sure you leave an imprint on the world, and the world knows you were here. I believe there is more for you. I believe you can have it all, but that lies within your decision to be.

Be the person you know you can, and then work like hell to get there!

ABOUT THE AUTHOR

 Ben Lang set himself apart as one of the preeminent real estate professionals in the industry today. With over 1,000 closed real estate transactions under his belt, Ben is a true success story that embodies dedication and hard work. With his focus on education and ongoing development, Ben is at the top of his game – and continues to raise the bar for others in his field. His commitment to personal and professional growth led him to become a certified coach, public speaker, and national trainer with the John Maxwell Certified Leadership Team in 2014.

Ben graduated Summa Cum Laude with a Psychology degree from the University of Rochester. His expertise lies in applying his knowledge of human behavior to sales strategies, which enables him to be adept at training teams and working with clients. A passionate professional,

Ben has earned an impressive array of certifications and designations, including SRS, CDPE®, SFR®, and ABR®, as well as his Broker's License.

Ben took the real estate industry by storm during the short sale boom in the 2009-2012 market and is known as an innovative, tech-savvy, real estate expert with the unique ability to understand and navigate rapidly changing markets. His success has been largely attributed to his unwavering commitment to quality customer service, coupled with his mastery of listing homes; typically selling 60+ listings per year.

With his mission rooted in professional development, Ben brings enthusiasm and energy as well as decades of experience to every event, as a leader, trainer, or participant. He believes strongly in the power of education and uses his own background to train agents nationwide on topics such as the psychology of sales, listing strategies, and how to leverage technology for maximum impact. With a knack for staying ahead of market and technology trends while helping others reach their goals, Ben continues to be a leader in the real estate industry. He has served as a Club Wealth Coach, spoken at various engagements, and is currently Growth CEO Coach. Whether through podcasts, speaking engagements, or one-on-one coaching sessions, Ben continues to offer his invaluable insights –

allowing him to continue his role as a leader in the real estate industry.

His drive, professionalism, and strong business acumen have helped him reach top levels of success, as he strives to lead others in a similar direction. Despite facing several setbacks in life, Ben has found success through resilience; witnessing firsthand how failure can be used as an opportunity for growth. His commitment to excellence and ability to turn adversity into opportunity serves as an example of what's possible when you don't give up on yourself or your dreams.

Ben is a true success story that embodies dedication and hard work. No matter what obstacle he may face, Ben continues to be at the forefront - inspiring individuals with his tenacity, passion, and commitment to excellence; a living testament of success that proves the sky's the limit. Ben's mission is to continue leading real estate agents to greater heights and ultimately change the face of the industry for decades to come. As an exemplary leader and a true role model for aspiring real estate professionals, Ben has earned his place at the top of the real estate industry. His stellar track record as a real estate coach, public speaker, and national trainer have allowed him to help shape the future of the industry, and his tireless devotion towards helping others achieve their goals have made him a trusted source within the real estate industry and beyond.